Football

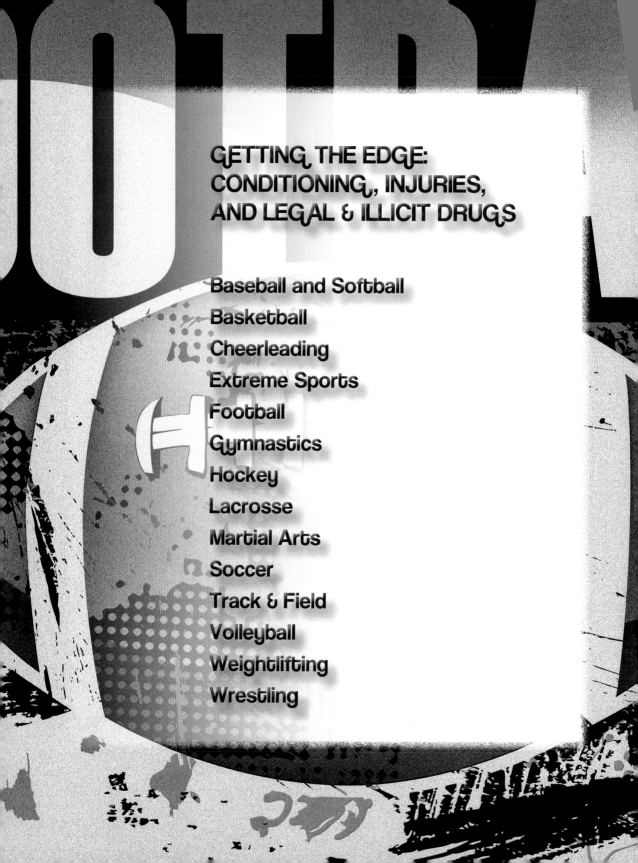

GETTING THE EDGE: CONDITIONING, INJURIES, AND LEGAL & ILLICIT DRUGS

Football

by J.S. McIntosh

MC

Mason Crest

MASON CREST
450 Parkway Drive, Suite D
Broomall, Pennsylvania 19008
(866) MCP-BOOK (toll free)
www.masoncrest.com

9 8 7 6 5 4 3 2

Library of Congress Cataloging-in-Publication Data

McIntosh, J. S.
  Football / by J. S. McIntosh. — 1st ed.
      p. cm.
  Includes bibliographical references and index.
  ISBN 978-1-4222-1733-7   ISBN (set) 978-1-4222-1728-3
  1. Football—Juvenile literature. I. Title.
  GV950.7.M36 2010
  796.33—dc22
                                    2010007230

Produced by Harding House Publishing Service, Inc.
www.hardinghousepages.com
Interior Design by MK Bassett-Harvey.
Cover Design by Torque Advertising + Design.
Printed in the USA by Bang Printing.

The creators of this book have made every effort to provide accurate information, but it should not be used as a substitute for the help and services of trained professionals.

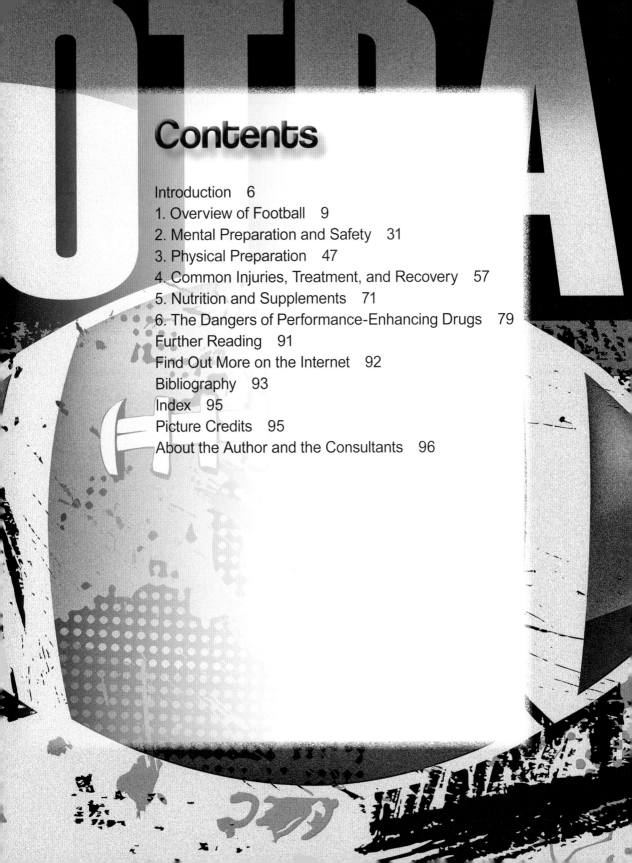

Contents

Introduction

GETTING THE EDGE: CONDITIONING, INJURIES, AND LEGAL & ILLICIT DRUGS is a four-teen-volume series written for young people who are interested in learning about various sports and how to participate in them safely. Each volume examines the history of the sport and the rules of play; it also acts as a guide for prevention and treatment of injuries, and includes instruction on stretching, warming up, and strength training, all of which can help play-ers avoid the most common musculoskeletal injuries. Each volume also includes tips on healthy nutrition for athletes, as well as information on the risks of using performance-enhancing drugs or other illegal substances. GETTING THE EDGE offers ways for readers to healthily and legally improve their performance and gain more enjoyment from playing sports. Young athletes will find these volumes informative and helpful in their pursuit of excellence.

Sports medicine professionals assigned to a sport with which they are not familiar can also benefit from this series. For example, a football ath-letic trainer may need to provide medical care for a local gymnastics meet. Although the emergency medical principles and action plan would remain the same, the athletic trainer could provide better care for the gymnasts after reading a simple overview of the principles of gymnastics in GETTING THE EDGE.

Although these books offer an overview, they are not intended to be comprehensive in the recognition and management of sports injuries. They should not replace the professional advice of a trainer, doctor, or nutrition-ist. The text helps the reader appreciate and gain awareness of the sport's history, standard training techniques, common injuries, dietary guidelines,

and the dangers of using drugs to gain an advantage. Reference material and directed readings are provided for those who want to delve further into these subjects.

Written in a direct and easily accessible style, GETTING THE EDGE is an enjoyable series that will help young people learn about sports and sports medicine.

—*Susan Saliba, Ph.D., National Athletic Trainers' Association Education Council*

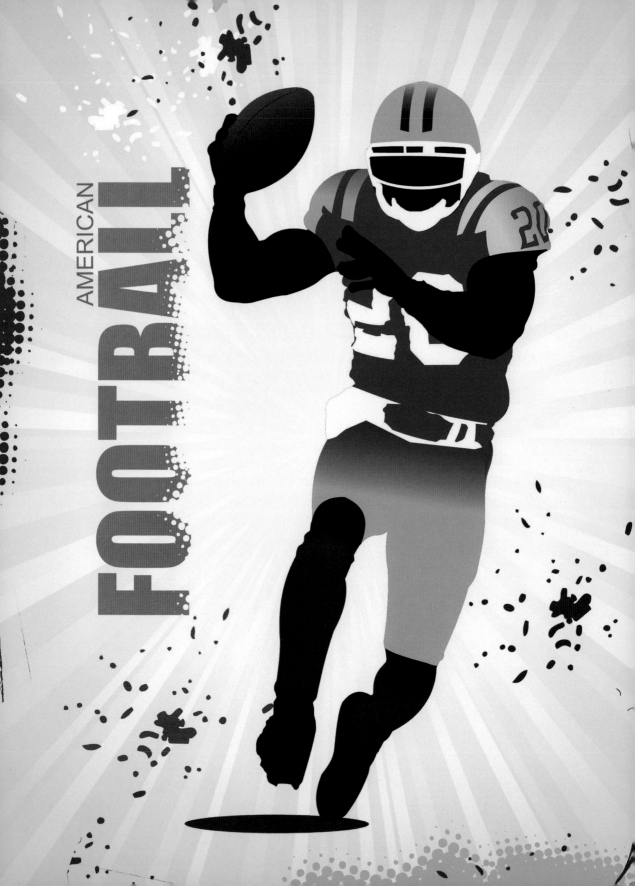

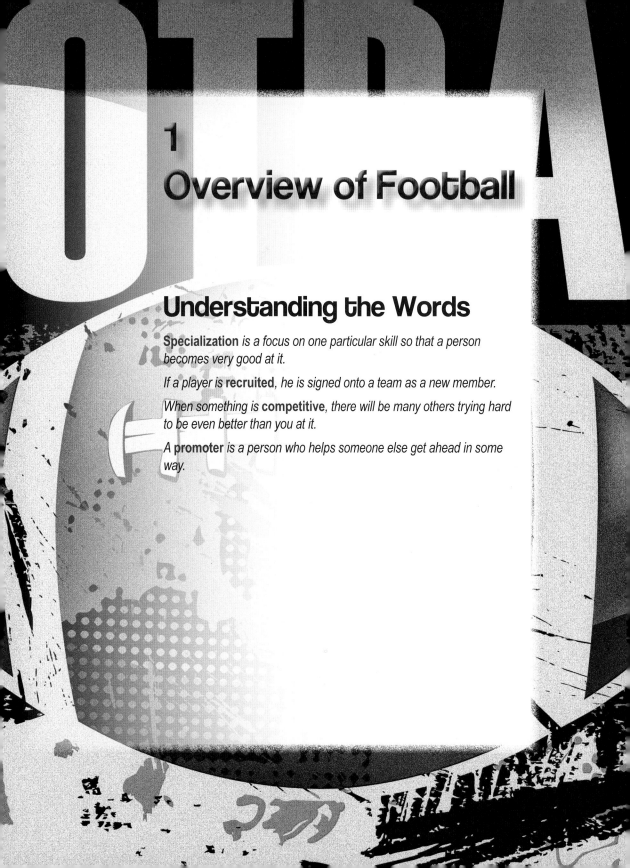

1 Overview of Football

Understanding the Words

Specialization is a focus on one particular skill so that a person becomes very good at it.

If a player is **recruited**, he is signed onto a team as a new member.

When something is **competitive**, there will be many others trying hard to be even better than you at it.

A **promoter** is a person who helps someone else get ahead in some way.

The basics of football are simple: two teams run an oval ball up and down a field. You keep score: the team that runs that leather ball to the other side the most often wins. The specifics of football, on the other hand, are complicated. The 2009 book of NFL rules is 300 pages long (compared to the soccer rule book which is a slim 150). There are specific guidelines for everything in football, from passes to the opening coin toss.

> **DID YOU KNOW?**
> The term "bowl" still used today for big post-season football matches came from the bowl-shaped stadium where the first of these matches was held— the Rose Bowl in Pasadena, California.

Beyond Common Sense: Staying Safe

The guidelines for staying safe and doing your best are similar. Sports safety seems simple: eat right, sleep right, train hard, and tell your doctor if you break a bone. These are things everyone knows, right?

On another level, though, staying safe and training hard aren't nearly as simple as you might think. Doctors spend years in medical school learning how to heal the injured. NFL teams hire sports psychologists, specialists in maintaining high morale and a responsible outlook for their teams. NFL teams spend thousands each year hiring safety professionals. Sports wellness and injury prevention require more than common sense.

The Origins of Football

FROM THE IVY LEAGUE TO SUPER STADIUMS

What Americans call football developed from British soccer and rugby in the 1820s. East-coast colleges were the first to have official games. Football was a rough sport during its beginnings in America, so rough that Harvard banned football in 1860.

Many of the nineteenth-century rules may seem strange to us now. For instance, a team had three downs to make five yards for a first down, which is why our modern gridiron is marked by five-yard sections. In the original game of football, players could not tackle a runner below the waist. The point system was also different: a touchdown was worth two points, a conversion added four more, and a field goal was worth five points. Several rule changes were put into place in the 1880s, but probably the most important was the introduction of the legal forward pass. When it became legal to throw the ball forward, an entirely new method of advancing the ball was born, and

This image of two Columbia football players from 1916 shows how different uniforms were then.

as a result, players became more specialized in their roles, as the different positions on the team required different skill sets. Thus, some players are primarily involved in running with the ball (the running back) while others specialize in throwing (the quarterback), catching (the wide receiver), or blocking (the offensive line).

College football quickly spread west. The university of Michigan adopted it in 1870, and Washington and Lee in 1873. The Rose Bowl, the first post-season match between teams, began in 1902.

CHANGES IN THE GAME

Football has frequently changed. The early twentieth century brought new rules and maneuvers: John Heisman introduced the forward pass in 1902. (His name is still found on the famous trophy that awards the best college football player of the year.) The "flying wedge" formation was another addition to football that allowed for a group, or wedge, of large blockers to protect the receiver of a kickoff. The flying wedge caused so many injuries and even deaths that President Theodore Roosevelt complained about it, and it was banned in 1920. The same year, the American Professional Football Association was formed; two years later, it was renamed the National Football League (NFL.)

One of the biggest differences between football now and in the 1920s is in equipment and clothing. In the early twentieth century, football players wore bulky uniforms and tight leather helmets, which looked similar to the helmets fighter pilots used. Some players refused to wear their helmets, however; they considered them unmanly.

With the advent of free substitution rules in the 1940s and 1950s, teams could deploy separate offensive and defensive "platoons," which led to even

greater **specialization** in players' skills. In less than one hundred years, football had grown from a college sport to be America's most popular sport.

By the 1960s, football looked and played pretty much like we know it today. In 1967, the Green Bay Packers defeated the Kansas City Chiefs in the first Super Bowl (then known as the AFL-NFL World Championship). Then, in the 1960s, television created an important football institution: the living room

Each player on a football team specializes in a certain task. The center, shown in this image with the ball, snaps the ball to the quarterback at the beginning of each play.

football game. Fans from around the country packed around TV sets to cheer for their favorite team, and football grew in popularity because of how accessible it had become.

By 2002, thirty-one teams were in the NFL. College football was also still popular.

CHANGES TO THE PLAYING FIELD

The football field has had its own share of changes and modifications. Since the nineteenth-century, football had been played outside on grass. Grass needs to be constantly maintained, though. It needs to be cut and patched; painted stripes kill it. Because of this, in the 1960s, football stadiums turned

Modern footballs look very different from the first ball used in American football games. The first balls were rounder—more similar to soccer balls than the familiar footballs of today.

DID YOU KNOW?

Astroturf® was invented in 1965. A year later, the Houston Astrodome was the first to use it.

to a synthetic material called Astroturf®. Astroturf cost more to put in, but it was cheaper to maintain. Today, many colleges and even high schools also use Astroturf for their football fields.

There are some downsides to Astroturf. Players frequently complained of "turf burn," since synthetic grass isn't as forgiving to falls or slides as natural grass planted in soil. In a study of 965 NFL players done in 1996, 96 percent of the players agreed that Astroturf caused more injuries than grass. So the company that makes Astroturf improved it by adding more padding and shock-absorbing layers. FieldTurf® was created in 1999 and offered softer cushioning by using a blend of sand and pieces of ground rubber. An even safer artificial field has been created using Astro-Play®, which uses rubber cushioning without sand.

Although artificial fields were met with criticism at first, they have become nearly the norm. By 2002, four pro-football teams, Dallas, Detroit, Philadelphia, and Seattle, had artificial playing fields. In that same year, 2000 schools in the U.S. had some form of artificial fields down for their teams.

DID YOU KNOW?

The modern football field is 360 feet (109.7 m) long and 160 feet (48.8 m) wide.

TOUCHDOWN

TOUCHDOWN

10 20 30 40 50

10 20 30 40 50 40 30 20 10

Coaching Legends

Players aren't born champions and teams don't achieve greatness over night; they need the guidance and wisdom of coaches. Vince Lombardi and Paul "Bear" Bryant demonstrated how victory is found off the playing field.

Vince Lombardi was born in Brooklyn in 1913. His list of achievements is as impressive as his attitude. From the beginning Lombardi held an aggressive approach to football. "Winning isn't everything," he once said to a player. "It's the only thing." Lombardi coached the Green Bay Packers to win conference titles six times, the NFL title five times, and won the first two Super Bowls in 1967 and 1968. He retired in 1968, only to return the following year. In his comeback, he coached the Washington Redskins, earning them their first winning record in fourteen years. In 1971, Lombardi was inducted to the Professional Football Hall of Fame, and the Super Bowl Championship trophy is now named the Vince Lombardi Super Bowl Trophy. In 2000, television network ESPN called Lombardi the "Coach of the Century." Lombardi showed that success in football is in the mind as much as the field, and winning is a mental accomplishment as well as a physical one.

If Lombardi represented the cutthroat aspect of winning football, then Paul "Bear" Bryant represents the need for respect in the game. He won the nickname "Bear" by wrestling a flesh-and-blood carnival bear for money. His football career started on the field in 1934 when he played an undefeated Alabama team. He moved to catcher at Maryland, Kentucky, and Texas before returning to Alabama to coach their college team. From 1958 to 1968, Coach Bryant won six national championships, thirteen Southeastern Conference titles, and twenty-four straight Super Bowl games. By the time his career was over, he had been the most successful coach of all time for a major college, winning 323 victories.

Winning wasn't all that made "Bear" Bryant famous. He was also known for his high respect for the game and good sportsmanship. A sign in his office said, "Be good or be gone." Coach Bryant instructed his players to act and dress like gentlemen. He said that after flooring an opponent with a crushing tackle, a member of the Crimson Tide was expected to extend a hand to the fallen payer. "I have tried to teach them to show class, to have pride, and to display character. . . . I think football—winning games—takes care of itself if you do that."

High school football has some different rules from college or professional games, for example, the quarters are 12 minutes rather than 15 and kickoffs take place at the kicking team's 40-yard line instead of the 30-yard line.

DID YOU KNOW?

If you were raised in most parts of the world (including Europe and South American), you would call soccer football. Football is the term for soccer (and sometimes rugby) for every country except America and Canada.

Basic Football Rules

As with any competitive sport, football has many rules. There are even differences between the rules for college and professional level football games. Officials must take classes to study and learn these rules so they are able to govern games accurately.

Despite the variety of rules, there are some basic rules that apply to all competition levels.

Pigskin?

You may hear a football called a "pigskin," but the balls are not made from pigs. The NFL and most NCAA balls are made from cowhide leather, while younger children often play with rubber balls.

The Ball

All football games are played with a ball shaped sort of like an egg with pointy ends (called a prolate spheroid shape). Footballs are made of a rubber or polyurethane bladder inside a covering of leather or rubber. This covering is textured, and laces are added along one side to allow for better grip. Before play, the bladder must be filled with air. The size of the ball will depend on the level of play—NFL balls are slightly larger than NCAA and high school balls, which in turn are larger than the balls used by children under the age of 13.

The Field

A football field is 100 yards long and 53 yards wide, with a 10-yard end zone at each end. The total length of the field is therefore 120 yards long. During an offensive possession, a team tries to get the ball into the opponent's end zone to score a touchdown. Out of bounds is marked by a white line—when a player steps over this line, play stops.

The 100 yards between the end zone lines are marked with lines every five yards and numbers every ten yards. From left to right the field reads 10, 20, 30, 40, 50, 40, 30, 20, 10. Every yard is also marked with dash, which are used to keep track of a team's movement down the field.

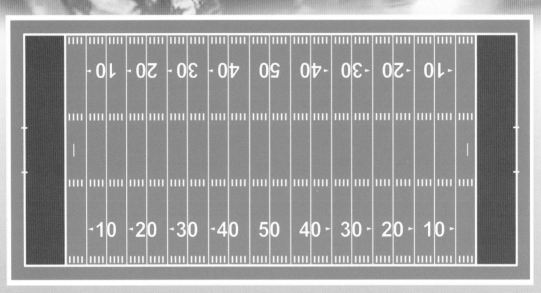

American football is played on a field that measures 360 by 160 feet (109.7 by 48.8 m). The numbers on the field indicate the number of yards to the nearest end zone.

Goal posts at both ends of the end zones are targets for field goals and extra point attempts. Kicking the ball through the posts, or uprights, earns a team three points for a field goal and one point for an extra point after a touchdown.

The Team

Each team is composed of an offense, a defense, and a special teams unit. Each unit is made up of 11 players.

OFFENSE

The team with possession of the ball is the offense. Only certain players on the offense can legally handle the ball: the quarterback, the wide receivers, the tight ends, and the running backs.

Quarterback

The quarterback is the leader of the team. He throws or hands off the ball and explains each play to the team.

Center

The center snaps the ball to the quarterback at the beginning of each play. After the ball has been snapped, the center blocks the defense to help protect the quarterback from being "sacked."

Guards & Tackles

There are two guards and two tackles that work to stop the defense in order to protect the quarterback.

Wide Receivers

Two to four wide receivers run up the field and catch balls thrown by the quarterback.

Running Backs

One or two running backs take the ball directly from the quarterback in a "hand off," and try to run the ball down the field.

Tight Ends

One of two tight ends stop the defense, but can also catch passes from the quarterback.

DEFENSE

The defense is on the field to stop the offense from moving the ball down the field. Their ultimate goal is to prevent the offense from scoring.

Linebackers

Linebackers defend against passes and runs. They also attempt to tackle the quarterback before he gets rid of the ball, called a "sack."

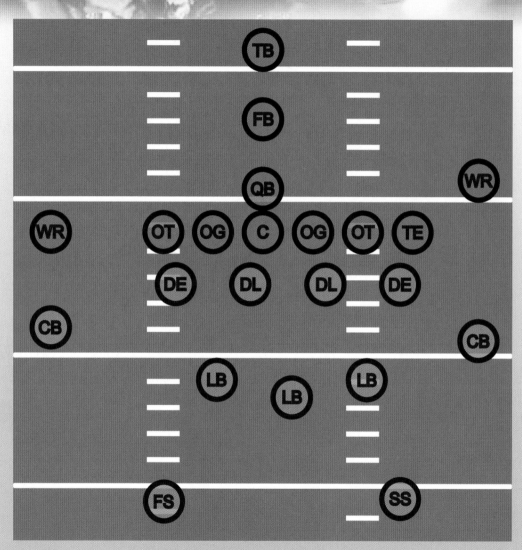

This diagram shows typical offensive and defensive formations. The offense (blue) consists of the quarterback (QB), fullback (FB), tailback (TB), wide receivers (WR), tight end (TE), and offensive linemen (C, OG, OT). The defense (red) consists of the defensive line (DL, DE), linebackers (LBs), cornerbacks (CB), strong safety (SS) and free safety (FS).

Ends and Tackles

Ends and tackles, called the defensive line, go up directly against the offensive line.

Cornerbacks and Safeties

Cornerbacks and safeties try to stop the wide receivers from catching passes. They also help to stop running backs from running the ball up the field.

SPECIAL TEAMS

The special teams come onto the field during kicking plays— punts, field goal attempts, or extra point plays. The most important players are the punter, the kicker, the holder and the long snapper.

Punter

The punter punts the ball when his team has reached the end

The holder is a member of the special teams unit.

of their possession of the ball (the fourth down). The ball is snapped to the punter, who catches, drops and then kicks the ball without letting it hit the ground.

Kicker

The kicker, or placekicker, handles the kicks that are taken off of the ground. The kicker kicks the ball during kickoffs, extra point attempts and field goal attempts.

Holder

The holder receives the ball from the snapper and places it into a good kicking position for the kicker.

Long Snapper

The long snapper is a specialized center, who makes longer snaps needed for punts or field goal attempts.

Gunner

Gunners run downfield to try and tackle the player from the other team who is returning the punt or kick.

The Fastest Touchdown

Homer Hazel, kickoff player for Rutgers, scored a touchdown on Villanova's team a whole eight seconds into the first quarter. He kicked off the ball into the end zone, where a Villanova player fumbled the ball. Hazel ran down the entire field and covered the ball, which was still in the end zone, with his body.

Walter Camp

Walter Camp is known as the father of modern football. He played football in college for Yale, but he is best known for his innovations to football rules. The modern system of downs, the modern point system, and the way in which players are arranged before plays start are all creations of Walter Camp. By the time he passed away in 1925, he had written 30 books and more than 250 magazine articles about football.

Punt or Kick Returner

The returners catch punts or kick-off kicks and attempt to run the ball back toward the opponent's end zone. The farther the returner can run, the better the field position when the offense steps onto the field. Better field position gives the offense a greater chance of scoring while they have possession.

Moving the Ball

The team with the ball has "possession," and it will try to get the ball down the field and into the opponent's end zone in order to score a touchdown. To move the ball, players can run with it or pass it.

A team has four chances, known as downs, to move the ball ten yards. A "down" is started with the snap of a ball and ends when the possessing team is stopped by the defense through a sack, a tackle, or an incomplete pass. An incomplete pass occurs when the quarterback throws the ball forward, but no one on either team catches it.

When a team successfully moves ten yards, they get a first down, which means they are given four more downs to move the ball another ten yards.

As long as a team keeps reaching this ten-yard goal, it retains possession and can keep moving towards the other team's end zone. If the team successfully carries the ball into the other team's end zone, a touch down (worth six points) is scored.

When a team is within ten yards the end zone, there are no more first down chances. The team must either score or lose possession of the ball. If there is no score after three downs, a team will usually choose to attempt a field goal to at least earn three points. Most kickers can kick a field goal from about 50 yards away, so teams will sometimes choose to attempt a field goal on the fourth down when they are within field goal range. The 35-yard line is usually considered field goal range (because the kicker stands further away than the line of scrimmage).

The punter usually comes out to punt the ball when a team fails to reach ten yards after three downs. The team is allowed to try and reach a first down in the fourth down, but most teams punt in order to give the other team worse field position.

Game Length

College and NFL games are one hour long, divided into four 15-minute quarters. The teams switch direction every quarter. High school games are usually shorter, typically with four 12-minute quarters.

OVERTIME

If the teams are tied after standard, or regulation, time, then the game might go into overtime. Overtime rules depend on the level of play. NFL games use

sudden death rules in overtime, which gives the win to the first team able to score during the extra time. There is a strong advantage for the team that wins the coin toss to determine first possession. If neither team has scored after an extra fifteen minutes, the game ends in a tie. During important games (e.g. playoffs), play will continue until a team scores.

College overtime rules allow each team equal opportunity to score. Each team starts on the opponent's 25-yard line and tries to score. Whichever team ends the overtime with more points is the winner. If neither team scores in the first overtime period, overtime continues in the same manner until a winner can be declared.

Penalties

There are many possible penalties in football. Referees throw yellow flags to indicate that a rule has been broken. The referees then talk to determine which team was at fault and what the yardage penalty will be.

Every rule carries a specific yardage penalty, usually somewhere between five and fifteen yards. When a team gets a five-yard penalty, the line of scrimmage (where each play begins) is pushed back and the team must now move fifteen yards to reach a first down.

CHANGES TO PENALTY RULES

Over the years many rules have been added to football to protect players. For example, a fair catch violation protects a receiver of a punt or kickoff; so long as he waves his hands, other players can't touch him. There are many illegal plays: grabbing a player's mask, hitting passers or kickers after they have the ball, hitting players hard from behind (clipping), or spearing, in which a player drives his helmet into an opponent who is on the ground. General precautions against unsportsmanlike conduct also exist.

Scholarship in Football

With over 75,000 participants on college and university teams, there are exciting opportunities for football players both on and off the court. The best high school players are **recruited** to nationally recognized college teams. Over thirty college athletic departments may seek after a gifted high-school athlete. Those schools receive national television exposure, which increases an athlete's chances of achieving what's probably his biggest dream: playing professional football.

The NCAA (National Collegiate Athletic Association) controls recruiting and eligibility for foot-

Super Bowl Ads

The big game isn't the only reason people watch the Super Bowl. It only took a few Super Bowls for corporations to start producing big-budget 30-second commercials. Advertisements between games have become as much a part of the football experience as popular musical artists performing at halftime. In a 1973 ad, Farrah Fawcett lovingly spreads Noxzema shaving cream onto Quarterback Joe Namath. In honor of the George Orwell novel, Apple televised an ad with futuristic overtones in 1984. Some non-sports fans even watch the Super Bowl **just** for the commercials! Super Bowl ads are now part of American culture.

ball scholarships. The largest colleges, which are in Division I-A, can have up to eighty-five players on football scholarships. Major schools with smaller programs in I-AA are allowed sixty-three. These scholarships are so **competitive** that some schools do not use their full number.

If you're a football player, don't assume you don't have to work to get good grades too in high school. Only one in ten high school players receive a full football scholarship, and even then, academic excellence is still important to college admissions. The lowest accepted high school grade point average is 2.0 (a C average). The NCAA requires that players maintain a similar GPA while they are in college.

These numbers may make playing college football seem like a distant dream—but there is much you can do to increase your chances of recruitment:

- Avoid injury and maintain good grades in the classroom.

- Specialize: Coaches want players who fill a special task in their teams, whether it's a player with an exceptional kickoff or a knack for pulling off unusual plays. Make recruiters aware of these skills on the field. Play every game like a recruiter is watching (after all, you never know).

- Your coach should act as your **promoter**; ask him to call colleges or even arrange tryouts with college recruiters.

- In the end, you are your best promoter. You can contact colleges and schedule campus visits. Also, you can update colleges on broken records, exceptional games, or if you earn any honors. Be determined, consistent, and persistent.

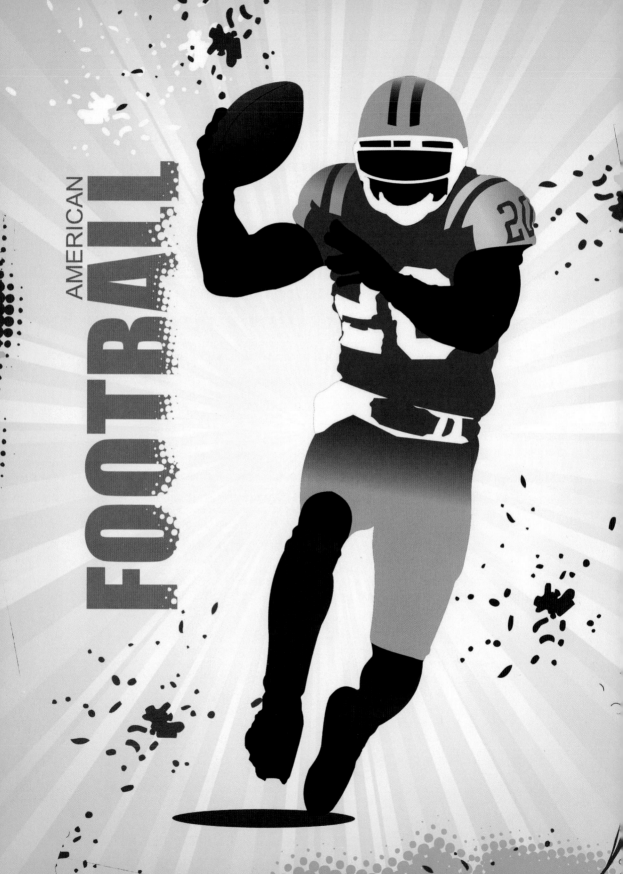

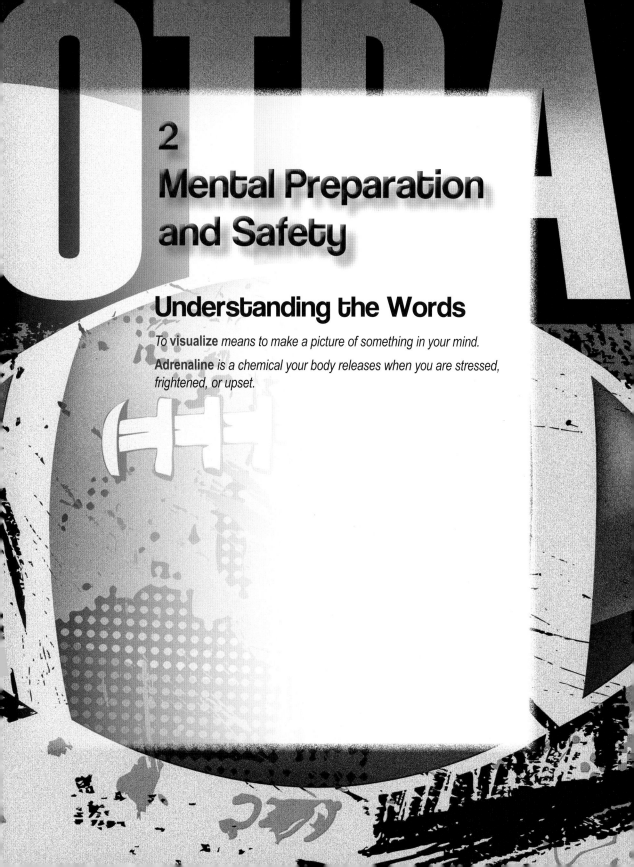

2
Mental Preparation and Safety

Understanding the Words

To **visualize** *means to make a picture of something in your mind.*

Adrenaline *is a chemical your body releases when you are stressed, frightened, or upset.*

We have all watched this scene in football movies: the coach is giving a speech to pump his players. He is encouraging them, getting them calm, then getting them excited. He gives the athletes this speech to get them into "the zone," a state of mental preparedness.

To prepare for a football game mentally is as important as being prepared physically. Think of the mind exercises as the equivalent to doing weight training weeks before a season or doing stretches right before a championship. Mental training is as necessary for winning as physical preparation.

At all levels of play, coaches have an important role in preparing their team and individual players both physically and mentally.

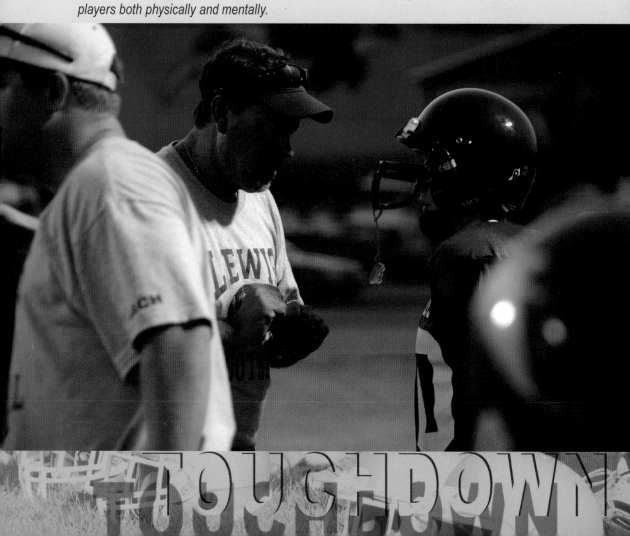

Sports Meditation

Baseball catcher Yogi Berra once said, "You can't hit the ball and think at the same time." Many proponents of sports meditation would agree with this statement. By meditating before a game, athletes are able to be in a heightened state of mindfulness during their games and instead of having to analyze the game play by play, they are able to increase the "intuitive" side of playing football. This means a player is not consciously analyzing what he is doing; instead of thinking about the game as a series of separate parts, he sees at as a whole, and his mind can make leaps that allow him to act before he is even aware that he has seen an opportunity.

A scientific study in 1974 measured how players did at the same set of tasks, which required coordination, after varying amounts of meditation. The group that meditated the most was best at the coordination tasks.

Coaches in real life as well as movies do many things to help their players get mentally fit. For instance, a coach many post in the shower room a negative newspaper column about his team to push his players for the next game. He may encourage his players to repeatedly **visualize** that they will overcome their opponents. Think of this as having the players watch an imaginary video of the game before it happens.

Getting in "the zone" has emotional and mental benefits (the more confident you feel, the better you're apt to play), but it also has physical

Personalities and Injury

Type-A personalities are individuals who have a higher amount of ambition, aggression, and competitiveness than Type-B personalities. People with Type-A personalities are more likely to be injured and usually take longer to recover than their more laid-back teammates. If you are more of a Type-A personality, then some extra relaxation exercises or meditation might help you. Just as in physical stretches and training, different amounts and kinds of preparation are needed for different players.

benefits. Sports psychologists have discovered that mental imagery is helpful for reducing injuries, while thinking negative thoughts leads to injuries. When players replace self-defeating ideas with more constructive thoughts, they not only make victory more likely, but they also create a safer environment.

One tool to use is positive reinforcement: assure yourself that you will be safe and always in control. Do your best to have fun, and be mindful of the changes to your playing you wish to make. Doing these mental exercises helps take away a win-at-all-costs attitude that can cause injuries. If a player reduces anxiety and controls emotions, he will play more confidently—and more safely.

Making time to relax is also important. Before-game relaxation exercises help lower muscular tension. These can also be done even while a game goes on. (This is why we sometimes see players on TV talk to themselves after an important play.) This is called "relaxed attention," staying aware while consciously trying to relax. Injuries are less common when anger and anxiety are controlled by relaxed attention. Decreasing negative emotions also reduces **adrenaline**, which can cause muscle tension and injury.

When coaches encourage players to get in the zone, it gets players in a mind-set where their mind and body are working together calmly, which in turn helps players get the best results on the field.

Projecting Victory: Mental Imagery

Setting goals is a major part of being mentally prepared. Before each game, you could set a goal for the amount of touchdowns

In between plays and when on the sidelines, players should use the time to gather their thoughts and refocus mentally.

Risk Control: Sports Superstitions

Many players have a set of rituals they do before they win a game. A quarterback might think that every time he listens to a specific song before a game, his team will win. A lineman may think if he eats a food related to the rival team's mascot, he will defeat that team. A coach has a pair of lucky pair of socks.

Psychologists are interested in sports superstitions. Psychologist George Gmelch made an important study on superstition in the 1970s where he found that when players had an easy task or they felt in control of what they had to do, they did not think luck was involved, and they felt no need for superstition. When the tasks became difficult, however, and players didn't feel they had as much control over outcomes, they developed superstitious behavior. Gmelch concluded that when athletes are in a situation where chance is involved and the stakes are high, they are more apt to believe in superstition.

Is superstition useful in sports? As the psychologist in the study discovered, superstition is our attempt to take control over something we really can't control. While we cannot prove whether or not the socks your coach wears makes a difference, we do know that superstition provides an extra confidence boost to the players. If you think you're more in control of elements of chance in a game, then you will play better.

A Career in Sports Psychology

If you think you'd like to work with athletes and have an interest in psychology, then sports psychology might be a good career option. A master's degree is required for most positions; to teach at the university level, you will need to go through more schooling to get a Ph.D. Many universities and colleges have sports psychology programs, and a few graduate schools offer specialized degrees. At the undergraduate level, you could take classes either in clinical psychology or counseling and then specialize on sports psychology later.

you want to make or the amount of points you want to make for the team. A player could also set longer-term goals; for example, a high-school player might want to move up to varsity status by the next season or be promoted to head quarterback. As you picture your goals in your mind, you are using mental imagery.

Of course, goals have to be realistic and achievable too. Some people would counter that statement, however, with the saying, "Shoot for the moon. If you miss, you'll end up in the stars." Joe Namath, star-quarterback of the New York Jets, is a football player that shot for the moon. He publically guaranteed that his AFL champions would beat the highly favored NFL champion, the Baltimore Colts, in Super Bowl III. An AFL team had never beaten an NFL team before—but by setting an ambitious goal, the NY Jets won the game 16–7.

Many think that when a team is closely matched, mental attitude is the deciding factor in winning. This is why many pro teams hire sports psychologists.

Before a game, a coach will discuss game tactics with the team. Drawing these game plans on a chalkboard helps each player visualize his role in each play.

Strategies vs. Tactics

Setting personal goals is known as a strategy, a word that means "a plan designed to achieve a particular long-term aim"; in other words, strategies help us achieve sports goals in the long term. "Tactics," on the other hand, are defined as "actions planned to achieve a specific end." Tactics are more specific, short-term plans, while strategies are long term.

The four major football tactics are:

- Fake and cut: When a receiver runs down the sideline, he fakes out the defensive team and then he cuts down to the middle of the field to receive a pass.

- Screen play: A quarterback makes a fake run and then throws the pass to a receiver in the backfield. A running back's screen helps the deception.

- Change of play: A play that was called in the huddle changes when the players are on the line. The center can call a line change at the last minute if he sees the defensive line move.

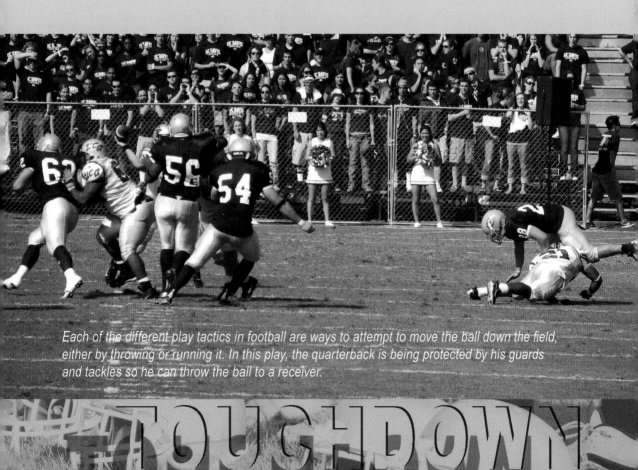

Each of the different play tactics in football are ways to attempt to move the ball down the field, either by throwing or running it. In this play, the quarterback is being protected by his guards and tackles so he can throw the ball to a receiver.

• Draw play: The quarterback drops back as though he's going for a pass, and then, when the opponent's linemen comes after him, he hands the ball to a lineman, who tries to run through the defensive gap.

Equipment

Football is the most dangerous of American team sports, which is why it should not be played without wearing appropriate equipment. Younger players are especially apt to get hurt because of the increased chance of injury to growing bones and muscle groups.

Standard football equipment includes a helmet with facemask, shoulder pads, padded pants and shoes with cleats.

For the face, players need to wear helmets and jaw pads. Foam-padded collars fit around the neck to protect against blows that jolt the head backward and cause whiplash. Shoulder pads worn beneath the jersey give football players their characteristic look, but they serve an important function: they absorb the shock from the point of impact. All players must also wear shin guards, jockstraps, and protectors.

Specialized players get specialized equipment. Quarterbacks wear flak jacket extensions below their shoulder pads. Linemen use flaps that cover the edges of their pads so their opponents cannot hold onto them. Receivers wear a special glove with sticky rubber palms.

Some football players wear specialized equipment to help in their specific roles. This wide receiver wears special gloves to help him make even difficult catches.

TOUCHDOWN

JV football coach Joe Maurelli tells this story about his experience with football and attitude:

Every high school is full of kids who can learn the team's offense and defense. But few teams have kids who are committed to the program, to forming a team relationship and having the attitude of never quitting no matter what the circumstance dictates. The teams that exhibit these traits always have a chance to win no matter what their talent level. Not only are these traits indicative of a successful season but also carry over into life. I try to teach each player there is life after football; football will comprise only a small portion of your life. So if my players exhibit the traits described above in everything they try, they will be very successful.

This year was a special year for the JV football team. I had a great group of kids who really came together as a team. Part of the reason was due to one individual . . . a running back (or RB, a person who runs the ball on offense) and listed as 5 feet tall, 100 lbs. By far he is our smallest guy (he was so small, he had to use two hands to hold the football). He never missed a practice, never talked back to the coaches, never asked about playing time. He was third string and would not get much playing time and knew this. But he loved playing football so much, that if he could only play by coming to practice, then that's what he would do. He knew he was too small to play, but told me he did not want to have any preferential treatment because of his size. So I treated him like any other player.

Since he was third string RB, it meant he ran the ball against our scout team (first string defense). He never hesitated to run right at our first string defense, and against my recommendation; I told him to dive down on the ground when he got near them because I was afraid he would get hurt. He would consistently run straight at guys who were 6 foot tall and 200 lbs, literally twice his size. Our defense would feel bad after some plays, but our guy would always get up and walk back to the huddle and continue on. During many practices, we would run drills with the Varsity players (all Running Backs would perform the same drills together). Most drills involved tackling the other Running Backs. He would jump in front of other guys and call out the first string Varsity players. Quickly, the varsity guys were asking me, who is this guy? He never really got the best of them, quite the contrary; they usually got the best of him. I could not believe his resolve and was inspired by his love of the game.

During the season I made sure to play everyone each game at least one play. So this guy did not get much playing time to say the least. He maybe got a couple of plays at most. But it did not matter to him. He got his fun in during practice.

Our last game of the year pitted us against our archrival. We had many players injured who could not play so in our pre-game meeting, I declared this little guy our team captain in order to inspire the team. The team really got pumped up. Then I learned one hour before the game, our starting Running Back could not play due to an injury. Now I needed to name a starting RB (we were already missing several RBs due to injury). So when we went through our pre-game walk through, I inserted our guy into the starting line-up. The entire team got fired up. He could not believe he would actually play in a game, but would start.

The first play of the game our player gets tackled very hard by the opposing team. The next play is the same result. It is obvious to me and the rest of the coaches we were too small and slow to keep up with the opposing team. We could be in for a long night. However, the next play changed the game, we scored a touchdown on a long run. Our guy played the entire game, catching passes, carrying the ball, blocking for our other running backs and even scoring his first ever touchdown. We won the game 46 to 6.

After the game I spoke to the opposing coach. He could not believe his team lost (their worst loss of the season). I could not believe we won (our best game of the season). It was truly a magical game and I truly believe it had mostly to do with one small guy inspiring our team. Every time he caught a pass or ran the ball, our team gave it a little extra. This guy loves the game of football. This love is what drove him to survive each practice, each drill, each hit. This love is what made him successful in his only (real) action during a game. His love taught me, reminded me, of my aspirations as a teen-ager. He inspired us all during our last game and touched me forever. He may have played his last game (the Varsity team cuts players) at the high school level, but because of his desire, commitment and team play, he will always remember scoring that touchdown and winning his last game. I know he is prepared to successfully continue his life after football and continue to strive for his dreams.

(Told on www.askalana.com/stories/passion.html.)

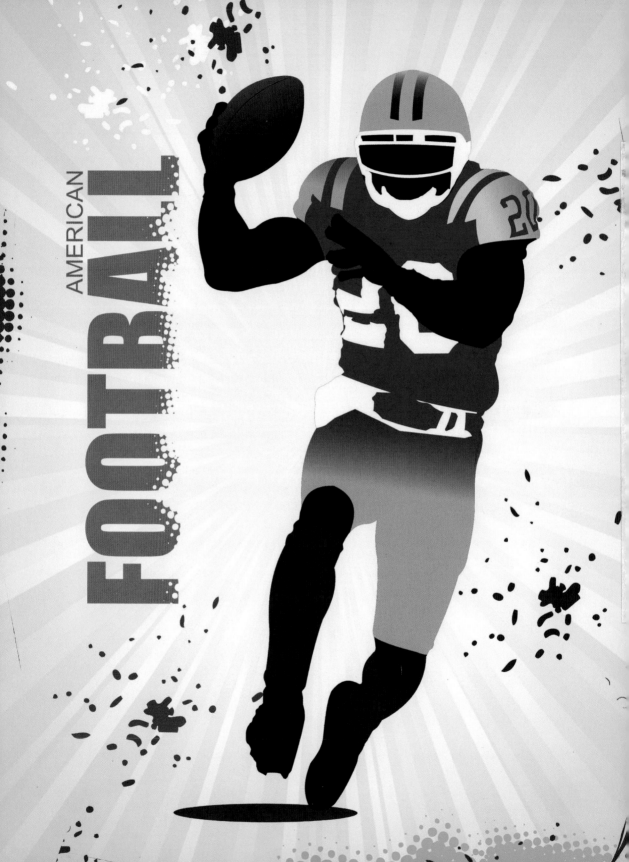

AMERICAN

FOOTBALL

3
Physical Preparation

Understanding the Words

Ligaments *are the tough, stretchy bands that fasten bones together.*

Aerobic *exercise brings more oxygen into your body by making your lungs and heart work harder.*

Mental preparation is important to sports, and so is the proper equipment. But obviously your body plays the starring role in any sport, including football. Getting your body in the best shape possible for football is vital to your success.

Rev-Up/Cooldown: How to Avoid Injuries and Increase Performance

You need to stretch your muscles before you play football or go through a rigorous practice. If you don't, your muscles will be less flexible, and you can suffer muscle strains or even worse, pull a muscle. The price of not setting

There are many different training techniques used by football teams. These players are using dummies to practice tackling and agility.

Stretching is an important part of warming up your body before a practice or game. Stretching should last 10–30 minutes depending on the temperature outside—muscles need a longer warm-up during cold weather.

aside time to stretch is much higher than the small amount of time needed to stretch before a game!

Warm-up exercises have many benefits. They stretch the **ligaments** and other connective tissues, and they raise the temperature inside muscles. Warm-ups rev up the body by making the heart beat faster and the lungs work harder. A warm-up brings more oxygen into the body. It's a way to send your body the message that it's time to start working in full gear. The ideal workout doesn't put too much of a strain on the body, though. You might think of a workout as the appetizer at a restaurant before the main course.

A warm-up makes your body more flexible and nimble on the field. It also allows you to have faster response times. Doing a warm-up also helps increase stamina; in other words, you can stay in the game longer and feel less fatigue.

For a game as demanding as football, the best stretching session lasts 10 to 15 minutes (or as long as 30 minutes in cold temperatures). Push-ups and sit-ups (known as calisthenic exercises) are also effective in the warm-up process. Exercises in which the whole team moves their hands, legs, or upper bodies quickly in unison (like jumping jacks) are also highly effective ways to warm up before a game.

The ideal warm-up position is lying down, so that players can slowly warm their ankle, knee, and hip joints. Then they can move to sitting or standing to do calisthenics.

Running during the off-season is a great way to keep in shape for football season. If you are on vacation near the ocean, try running on the beach.

EXERCISES FOR FLEXIBILITY

Some stretches are continuous motions, others should be held for a few seconds. All of these exercises are applicable to any sport, but they emphasize parts of the bodies used most in football. While these exercises are beneficial to all football players, each player should stretch the muscles they use most for a game. For example, a quarterback should concentrate on his throwing arm or shoulders; a lineman should stretch his neck and back.

Remember, every athlete has a different comfort threshold when it comes to stretching. What may be a comfortable stretch for one athlete may be harmful for another who is less flexible.

Shoulders, Chests, and Arms

1. Stretch arms upward and backward.

2. Stretch arms straight up; extend arms toward the sky one at a time.

3. Rotate arms forward in circles; move one up as the other descends.

4. Hold each elbow behind the head in a pulling motion.

5. Raise the arms shoulder level, pull them back, and hold the position.

Waist

Hold arms out to the side and swing them while you twist the torso back and forth.

Back, Abdomen, and Hip Muscles

While on your back, bend your knees toward your chest and make a cycling motion with your legs, as if you were riding a bicycle upside down.

Lower Back and Thighs

Touch your toes while standing or sitting.

Hips and Hamstrings

Sit with legs spread and knees locked. Bend forward and attempt to grasp each ankle. Take turns with each leg; hold the position for around ten seconds.

Knees and Ankles

Lie down and bring each individual knee toward the chest five times. Take turns with each leg and hold the position as you slowly rotate your foot.

> **DID YOU KNOW?**
> While you're a teenager, heavy weight training isn't a good idea. While your body is growing, it's likely to be damaged by this form of training.

Cooling Down

Safe football also requires a cool-down period after a game. If you set aside two to five minutes after a rigorous workout, you can reduce the chances you'll feel faint. Cooldowns slow the heart rate back to normal and return the body to its usual state. Walking, jogging lightly, and stretching again help your body recover after its been working hard. If you don't have time to jog or stretch, at least don't sit down immediately after a game. If you do, you may find you feel faint.

Off-Season Fitness

One of the best ways to avoid football injuries is to exercise all year long, not just when football is in season. Think of off-season strength conditioning as insurance against dangerous amounts of fatigue when football is back in season. Off-season fitness can be maintained by general **aerobic** exercise like running, swimming, or cycling. Off-season sports like indoor soccer, tennis, or racquetball can also be good aerobic exercise. Even regular one-on-one games of basketball will help your lungs and heart stay in shape.

Space Out Your Training

Training too much, without giving your body time to recover, can also cause injuries. Try not to train too many days in row. While this may not be possible for intense periods of training, in the off-season, space out difficult training days with days of rest.

Closer to the season, a football player should work on conditioning exercises that emphasize strength, speed, and endurance. He should pay attention to muscle groups that are used most in games. Pull-ups or sprinting will build and tone muscle mass, as well as increase endurance.

Training: How Much Is Too Much?
How Much Is Not Enough?

The Pop Warner Football program, an organization of about 400,000 football players from five to sixteen years old, requires football players to have fifty hours of training and conditioning before playing. Keep in mind this is for the average player. The emphasis on training should be on the quality and consistency of training rather than fitting an exact amount of hours in during the preseason time frame.

Players also need to avoid overtraining, which can happen at the start of football season. If you feel extra tired and your body shows signs of stress, you may be overtraining. Unusually poor performance is another sign that you're training too hard. While these problems are often temporary and can be reversed, it's better to avoid them altogether!

Using Video Games to Train for Football

Wired magazine's Chris Suellentrop tell this story to illustrate a new development in football training:

The situation was desperate for the Denver Broncos. On the first Sunday of the National Football League's 2009 season, with only 28 seconds left in the game, they trailed the Cincinnati Bengals 7-6. The ball was on the 13-yard line—their own 13-yard line. On second down, Broncos quarterback Kyle Orton heaved the ball downfield, only to see a Bengals defender deflect the pass away from the receiver. And then something remarkable, close to miraculous, happened. Instead of falling to the ground, the ball popped into the air and landed in the outstretched arms of Broncos wide receiver Brandon Stokley, who started racing down the field. All across America, in living rooms and basements and sports bars, people broke into cries of wonderment and delight, heartbreak and disbelief.

Then they witnessed something even more startling.

Just before he reached the end zone, with 17 seconds remaining, Stokley cut right at 90 degrees and ran across the field. Six seconds drained off the clock before, at last, he meandered across the goal line to score the winning touchdown.

For certain football fans, the excitement of a last-minute comeback now commingled with the shock of the familiar: It's hard to think of a better example of a professional athlete doing something so obviously inspired by the tactics of video-game football. When I caught up with Stokley by telephone a few weeks later, I asked him point-blank: "Is that something out of a videogame?" "It definitely is," Stokley said. "I think everybody who's played those games has done that"—run around the field for a while at the end of the game to shave a few precious seconds off the clock. Stokley said he had per-formed that maneuver in a videogame "probably hundreds of times" before doing it in a real NFL game. "I don't know if subconsciously it made me do it or not," he said.

Today's football players have an edge that no athletes before them have possessed: They've played more football than any cohort in history. Even with the rise of year-round training, full-contact practice time on the field hasn't increased—in fact, it has actually gone down, as coaches have tried to limit the physical punishment that the game exacts. But videogames, especially the ubiquitous Madden NFL, now allow athletes of all ages to extend their training beyond their bodies.

(From www.wired.com/magazine/2010/01/ff_gamechanger)

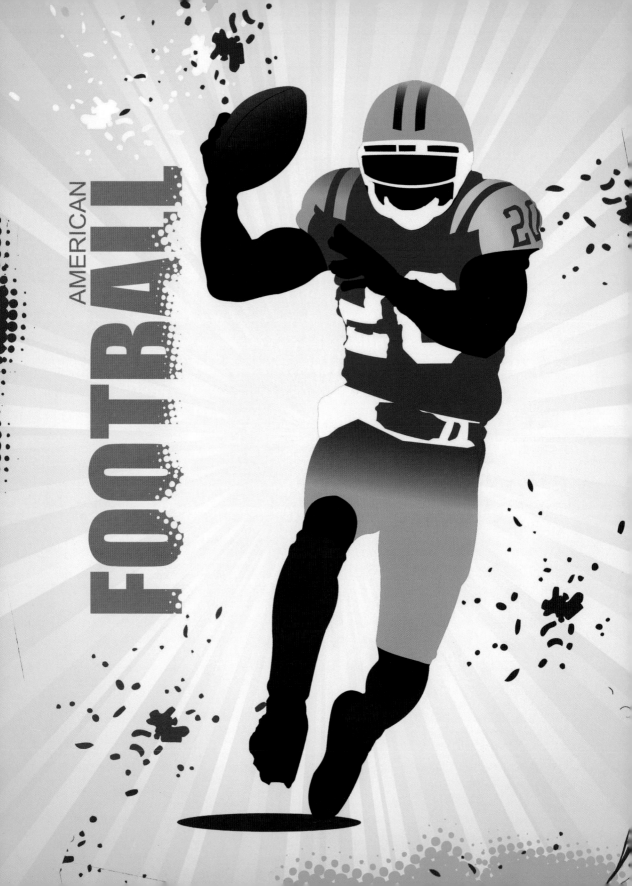

AMERICAN FOOTBALL

4
Common Injuries, Treatment, and Recovery

Understanding the Words

Something that is **acute** usually begins suddenly and is very serious.

Traumatic has to do with a serious injury or shock to the body.

Something that is **chronic** is an ongoing or recurring condition.

Rehabilitation is the process of getting something back into normal working order.

Your **hamstring** is the tendon behind your knee.

Every year brings 448,000 injuries to football players under the age of fifteen. While the NFL has the highest percentage rates of injury, adolescent players are especially vulnerable to injury because their bodies are still growing. In grade school, injuries are less common because game play is relatively tame. In high school, however, players are large, stronger, and faster—which means when they get hurt, the injury is apt to be more serious. Few football injuries are fatal, but in 2001, seven high-school athletes did lose their lives due to football injuries.

Injuries can be classified in one of two ways: **acute** injury and injury through overuse. When a player suffers from forceful impact during a game, we call this an acute **traumatic** injury. Overuse injury is more likely to be **chronic** and not quite so painful.

On the Field vs. On the Screen

Forty-six percent of players retired from football due to an injury, according to a Ball State survey of football players.

The intensity of impact that the typical football player endures is difficult to understand because television's bird's-eye view lacks an accurate perspective of the actual conditions on the field. Curt Marsh, a retired NFL player, described football's violence in the **San Francisco Chronicle**: "Think about it. . . . Our intent is to run into each other as hard as we can, 60 or 70 times a game, over and over again, trying to knock the other person down or move them out of the way. If someone asked you to do that for a living, you'd think they're crazy."

Types of Pain

There are many types of pain, and knowing which type you have is helpful when speaking to a coach or doctor. The two major kinds are similar to the classifications of injury: acute and chronic pain. Acute pain is localized, which means that we experience it in one location. Acute pain has been described as a stabbing or piercing feeling, more intense than chronic pain. Chronic pain feels more like a gentler, throbbing ache and usually lasts longer than acute pain. If you are injured, try your best to think of ways to describe your pain. Does it feel chronic or acute?

Many overuse injuries are specific to the different types of football players. A quarterback may have chronic pain in his wrist, while a wide receiver might overuse his ankle. The dull ache of overuse injury may seem less important than an acute injury (such as a broken bone), but these injuries also require medical attention.

In football, certain parts of the body are more likely to be injured.

Foot and Ankle

Foot and ankle injuries are common for all positions in football. Feet take large amounts of physical stress. Many players land on their heels instead of toes, which can cause acute pain. Football players often kick each other unintentionally in the process of the game.

Examples of Acute Traumatic Injuries

- contusions (bruises) caused by a direct hit. Contusions result in direct swelling—and possibly bleeding—in muscles or other tissues.
- sprains (when ligaments tear or stretch).
- strains (when muscles or tendons—the bands that connect muscles to bone—tear or stretch).
- abrasions (scrapes).
- lacerations (cuts to the skin that are deep enough to require stitches).
- fractures (when bone is cracked, broken, or shattered).

Fractures can be acute injuries, but they can also be caused by overuse. Football players often have stress fractures: tiny cracks in the bone's surface caused by constant physical stress. Receivers are especially vulnerable to stress factures in their feet and ankles because they frequently jump up for passes and then land hard. The chronic pain of a stress fracture can eventually lead to a limp. A doctor should be consulted even if the pain seems not very serious. The R.I.C.E. program should be used, with an emphasis on the R (rest.)

A sprained ankle is another common football injury. Quick changes of direction can overstress ligaments, pushing them out of their normal angles. Unless the injury is carefully monitored,

DID YOU KNOW?

The biggest factor for predicting whether a player will be injured on the field is his past injuries. Players who have been injured in the past year are 25–50% more likely to be injured again.

the sprain may recur later in the season. The closer a player follows his doctor's **rehabilitation** exercises, the lower the chance of an injury happening in the same place again.

Knees and Legs

Tackling causes knee and leg injuries. Quick turns and direct collision cause most of these injuries. The most common injuries for the knee and leg are sprains, strains, and dislocations. They range in seriousness from a bruised knee to a fractured leg. Some of the most common are:

• Knee sprains. The ligament in the leg is stretched or torn by the popping of the knee, which may cause a snapping sound and a feeling of deep pain.

• **Hamstring** sprain.

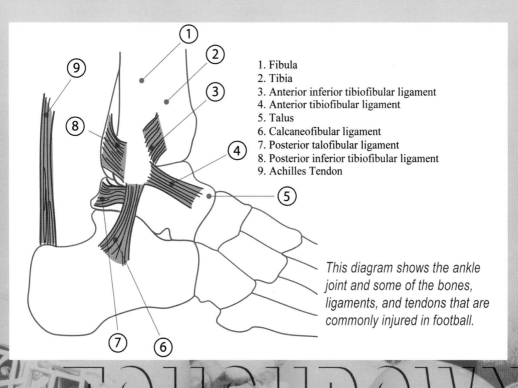

1. Fibula
2. Tibia
3. Anterior inferior tibiofibular ligament
4. Anterior tibiofibular ligament
5. Talus
6. Calcaneofibular ligament
7. Posterior talofibular ligament
8. Posterior inferior tibiofibular ligament
9. Achilles Tendon

This diagram shows the ankle joint and some of the bones, ligaments, and tendons that are commonly injured in football.

R.I.C.E.

Doctors have come up with an easy way to remember how to treat an injury: R.I.C.E. This stands for rest, ice, compression, elevation.

After an injury, spend 20 to 30 minutes resting. Apply ice to the injured area, wrap it in a compression bandage, and put it higher than the rest of your body.

- A dislocated kneecap (also called a patella). A hard tackle can knock the kneecap off to one side, which will cause a painful swollen bulge on one side of the knee. Walking is difficult with a dislocated knee, and a doctor is typically required to put the kneecap back into its proper position. Most players will wear a knee brace to prevent reinjury.

- Leg contusions and bruises. Players often cause contusions by hitting their helmets against another player's thigh. Compression and ice are used to treat these injuries, along with swimming and walking exercises, which make the muscles less tight.

DID YOU KNOW?

A strain involves a partial or full tear of the muscle or tendon and feels similar to a sprain but with more bruising.

- Leg fractures. These are extremely painful and can end a player's season. Crutches need to be used, and X-rays are usually required for a medical diagnosis.

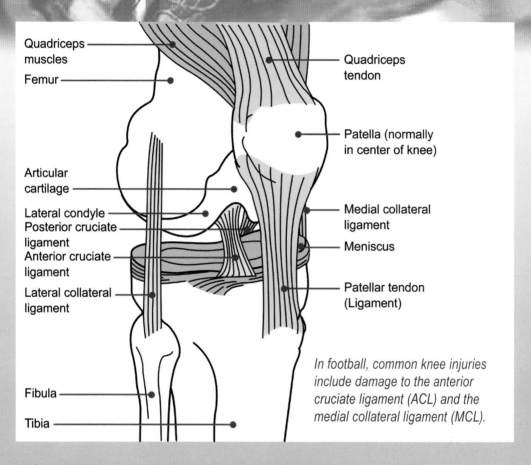

Quadriceps muscles

Femur

Articular cartilage

Lateral condyle
Posterior cruciate ligament
Anterior cruciate ligament
Lateral collateral ligament

Fibula

Tibia

Quadriceps tendon

Patella (normally in center of knee)

Medial collateral ligament

Meniscus

Patellar tendon (Ligament)

In football, common knee injuries include damage to the anterior cruciate ligament (ACL) and the medial collateral ligament (MCL).

Hip, Rib, and Back Injuries

Most injuries to the torso are bruises and strains, although hard impact could cause broken ribs. Quarterbacks suffer bruised or broken ribs when they are hit broadside while throwing a pass. Linemen commonly suffer back injuries as well, but their backs are usually sprained (not broken). Other injuries include:

• Hip pointer injuries. These are bruises at the upper ridge of the pelvis.

• Strained adductor muscles (which are located under the hips). This can be caused by moving sideways on the field.

- Rib injuries. These are painful, and X-rays are needed to determine if the rib is broken. Even if the fractured rib is not separated, you should allow for six weeks of rest in order to heal.

- Sprained backs. Players often use braces to recover from these.

- "Slipped" disk. A severe blow to the back may cause the disk between two vertebrae to bulge out of place, putting pressure on nerves and causing acute pain. Treatment includes medication, wearing a neck collar, traction, and sometimes surgery.

- Vertebrae fractures. These can occur if the back is bent backward after hard impact. A fracture is rare but dangerous. Recovery should take at least six weeks, and players with a minor fracture may need to wear neck braces until the bone heals, which may take up to six to eight weeks. In some cases surgery is required.

Pain: Your Mind-Set Matters

Athletes experiencing a great deal of pain from an injury can learn to control their pain with coping strategies. These include meditation, visualization, and positive thinking (discussed in chapter 2). Scientists did a study in which half of patients with back pain were given coping strategies and the other half were not. Those patients who were taught coping strategies dealt with pain much more easily than those who were given no instruction. Your mind-set is more important for your recovery than you may think!

Back and rib injuries are commonly the result of a hard tackle or an awkward fall.

Shoulders, Arms, and Wrists

Tackling and falling causes many shoulder, arm, wrist, and finger injuries. Since a defensive player tackles other players many times in a game, shoulder, arm, and wrist injuries are more common than others. These include:

- A separated shoulder. This results when a ligament tears at the end of the collarbone (or clavicle). The clavicle can be raised up slightly. The best treatment is rest and then strengthening exercises.

- A dislocated shoulder. This is a more serious injury than a bone separation. It involves the shoulder popping out of the socket because of loose ligament or torn cartilage. X-rays are needed to diagnose this. The injured players usually wear a shoulder sling for about three weeks. Only the most serious dislocations require surgery.

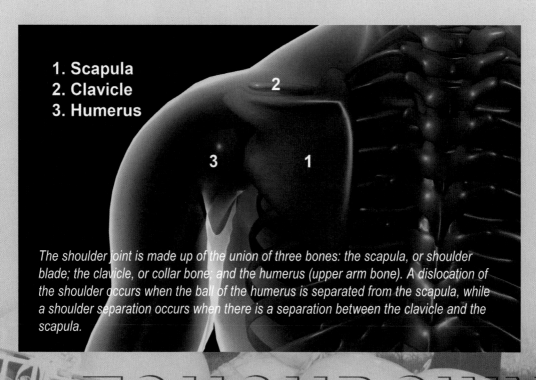

1. Scapula
2. Clavicle
3. Humerus

The shoulder joint is made up of the union of three bones: the scapula, or shoulder blade; the clavicle, or collar bone; and the humerus (upper arm bone). A dislocation of the shoulder occurs when the ball of the humerus is separated from the scapula, while a shoulder separation occurs when there is a separation between the clavicle and the scapula.

- Broken bones. These are often treated temporarily on the sideline with a splint. (Some players have finished games believing they were only suffering from a sprain.) X-rays are needed to diagnose broken bones, which will then be immobilized in a cast. Bone usually requires at least six weeks to heal.

Necks and Heads

Football players wear their big, bulky helmets to protect their necks and heads. The most serious injuries occur at these areas. These injuries usually happen while the heads of players are lowered, most often when a running back bends over to protect the ball. Neck injuries vary in severity, while head injuries are usually more serious. These injuries include:

- Stingers. When the nerves of the neck stretch too far, it causes a stinging pain and temporary numbness that is referred to as a stinger. While these symptoms are temporary, let your coaches or trainers know if you feel this way while playing.

- Whiplash. This occurs when a player's neck snaps backward, causing a sprain or strain in the neck. Doctors use neck collars or braces for recovery.

- Neck fractures. These involve the spinal cord and are very serious. A player with a neck fracture should not be moved, since doing so could cause paralysis or even death. That's why players on the ground need to stay where they are until emergency help arrives and the seriousness of the injury is determined. The neck may be supported with a brace and healed through exercise.

- Concussions. A concussion is an injury to the brain caused by a blow that usually causes a lack of consciousness. More than 90 percent of concussions are mild but all concussions can cause problems like

If a player lands awkwardly and a head or neck injury is suspected, his neck will be immobilized and he will be taken off the field on a stretcher to prevent further damage.

headaches, lack of alertness, fainting, and loss of short-term memory. If you've had any of these symptoms, you should stop playing immediately. Because concussions vary widely in their symptoms, X-rays are needed. A player should not play for up to four weeks after the symptoms disappear.

Coming Back After an Injury

Justin Duke knows how hard it is to come back after a serious injury—but he also knows that determination and faith are important parts of the healing process. After a serious head injury left him paralyzed in a wheel chair, it didn't look like he would ever play football again. But Justin proved everyone wrong, and three years later he ran out on the football field for his first game since his injury. "It might be a cliché," Justin said, "but being out there showed me that if you work hard enough, hold on to your faith and really want something, nothing is impossible. I know I could still be in a wheelchair today watching from the sidelines, but the dream of playing football again kept me going."

- Hematoma. A blow to the head could cause a fatal hematoma, which involves bleeding under the skull. If bleeding continues, pressure on the brain increases as well. Less severe hematomas clear up by themselves, but surgery may be required to remove blood clots. Players and coaches should assume that all head injuries are serious.

Football is a rough sport, and injuries are bound to happen. Physical and mental training can help protect against them, though, and proper care can make them less likely to happen again. Nutrition also plays an important role in keeping the football player's body strong.

AMERICAN

FOOTBALL

5
Nutrition and Supplements

Understanding the Words

Synthesis *means the process of putting something together.*

A **nutritionist** *is a person who specializes in helping people eat healthy diets suited to their individual needs.*

Eating well is crucial to an athlete's overall wellness. When we see gigantic linemen on ESPN with huge, bulky muscles we know those players have regulated their diets for years. Achieving remarkable amounts of muscle mass requires intense amounts of discipline. However, the benefits of maintaining healthy nutrition are greater than just being able to take down another player easier; a healthy diet will also lead to fewer injuries on the field.

Knowing what to eat as well as when to eat and how often is important. There are decisions to be made: What kind of diet can your body handle? Should you take dietary supplements?

Calorie Intake

Male high-school and college-level football players need to eat more than the average American. The Food and Drug Administration (called the FDA) states that the typical adult should eat 2,000 calories—but a football player, who is much more active and needs to build and maintain larger amounts of muscle mass, consume more than 4,000 calories. In some very intense preseason sessions, players who are at the top of their game may even consume up to 10,000 calories, five times more than an inactive person's diet! Remember, though: always consult your doctor or dietician before making any dramatic changes to your diet.

Power Food

One of the worst things a player could do who is trying to gain muscle mass and get lean is not eat. Knowing what to eat and when to eat it is important for training, especially when trying to tone muscles.

DID YOU KNOW?

Many sports dieticians recommend that football players not eat a few large meals each day, but instead, graze, which means eating smaller amounts of food more often. This gives your body the maximum amount of energy during training.

Daily required caloric intake varies depending on age, sex, and activity level.

Gender	Age (years)	Activity Level[b,c,d]		
		Sedentary[b]	Moderately Active[c]	Active[d]
Child	2–3	1,000	1,000–1,400[e]	1,000–1,400[e]
Female	4–8	1,200	1,400–1,600	1,400–1,800
	9–13	1,600	1,600–2,000	1,800–2,200
	14–18	1,800	2,000	2,400
	19–30	2,000	2,000–2,200	2,400
	31–50	1,800	2,000	2,200
	51+	1,600	1,800	2,000–2,200
Male	4–8	1,400	1,400–1,600	1,600–2,000
	9–13	1,800	1,800–2,200	2,000–2,600
	14–18	2,200	2,400–2,800	2,800–3,200
	19–30	2,400	2,600–2,800	3,000
	31–50	2,200	2,400–2,600	2,800–3,000
	51+	2,000	2,200–2,400	2,400–2,800

a These levels are based on Estimated Energy Requirements (EER) from the Institute of Medicine Dietary Reference Intakes macronutrients report, 2002, calculated by gender, age, and activity level for reference-sized individuals.   "Reference size," as determined by IOM, is based on median height and weight for ages up to age 18 years of age and median height and weight for that height to give a BMI of 21.5 for adult females and 22.5 for adult males.

b Sedentary means a lifestyle that includes only the light physical activity associated with typical day-to-day life.

c Moderately active means a lifestyle that includes physical activity equivalent to walking about 1.5 to 3 miles per day at 3 to 4 miles per hour, in addition to the light physical activity associated with typical day-to-day life

d Active means a lifestyle that includes physical activity equivalent to walking more than 3 miles per day at 3 to 4 miles per hour, in addition to the light physical activity associated with typical day-to-day life.

e The calorie ranges shown are to accommodate needs of different ages within the group. For children and adolescents, more calories are needed at older ages. For adults, fewer calories are needed at older ages.

Timing is important with eating and drinking water. A player should eat a small meal between a half-hour to an hour before he trains. Also, athletes should drink large amounts of water (20 ounces) one to two hours before a practice. While exercising, players should push smaller amounts of water into their system. Immediately after exercising, a small snack is a good idea, and around an hour after training, a player should have a larger meal.

Players should be eating as many carbohydrates as possible. These foods supply the body with energy. Pasta, rice, and bread are examples of

The food pyramid at www.mypyramid.gov gives advice for healthy diet choices and serving amounts.

GRAINS Make half your grains whole	VEGETABLES Vary your veggies	FRUITS Focus on fruits	MILK Get your calcium-rich foods	MEAT & BEANS Go lean with protein
Eat at least 3 oz. of whole-grain cereals, breads, crackers, rice, or pasta every day 1 oz. is about 1 slice of bread, about 1 cup of breakfast cereal, or 1/2 cup of cooked rice, cereal, or pasta	Eat more dark-green veggies like broccoli, spinach, and other dark leafy greens Eat more orange vegetables like carrots and sweetpotatoes Eat more dry beans and peas like pinto beans, kidney beans, and lentils	Eat a variety of fruit Choose fresh, frozen, canned, or dried fruit Go easy on fruit juices	Go low-fat or fat-free when you choose milk, yogurt, and other milk products If you don't or can't consume milk, choose lactose-free products or other calcium sources such as fortified foods and beverages	Choose low-fat or lean meats and poultry Bake it, broil it, or grill it Vary your protein routine — choose more fish, beans, peas, nuts, and seeds
For a 2,000-calorie diet, you need the amounts below from each food group. To find the amounts that are right for you, go to MyPyramid.gov.				
Eat 6 oz. every day	Eat 2½ cups every day	Eat 2 cups every day	Get 3 cups every day; for kids aged 2 to 8, it's 2	Eat 5½ oz. every day

Find your balance between food and physical activity
- Be sure to stay within your daily calorie needs.
- Be physically active for at least 30 minutes most days of the week.
- About 60 minutes a day of physical activity may be needed to prevent weight gain.
- For sustaining weight loss, at least 60 to 90 minutes a day of physical activity may be required.
- Children and teenagers should be physically active for 60 minutes every day, or most days.

Know the limits on fats, sugars, and salt (sodium)
- Make most of your fat sources from fish, nuts, and vegetable oils.
- Limit solid fats like butter, margarine, shortening, and lard, as well as foods that contain these.
- Check the Nutrition Facts label to keep saturated fats, *trans* fats, and sodium low.
- Choose food and beverages low in added sugars. Added sugars contribute calories with few, if any, nutrients.

carbohydrates, as well as fruits and vegetables. A football player's body needs plenty of carbohydrates, but he should avoid those that contain lots of white sugar, including sugary energy drinks; these make some athletes feel sick and give them cramps while working out.

After a workout, a football player should eat foods like chicken or tuna that are high in protein. These foods will help the body repair damaged muscles.

WATER

Before and after you work out, weigh yourself. If your body lost weight, drink a cup of water for every pound that you lost.

Dietary Supplements

A healthy diet is the best way to get the nutrients your body needs. You should only take supplements if for some reason you cannot get enough of something your body needs through the food you eat. If you don't absolutely have to take that extra pill, then don't!

VITAMIN AND MINERAL TABLETS

Football players need to get certain amounts of vitamins to perform at their best on the field. Ideally, a player should eat foods that have the right vitamins in them, since in general it is always best to get vitamins and minerals from their original source: food. Sometimes this isn't possible and most American's diets are not as balanced as they need to be. Most of the foods we eat, especially at restaurants, are highly processed and are not as rich in vitamins as they should be. For example, a fish sandwich at a fast-food restaurant will not have nearly as many Omega-3 fatty-acids as a fish bought fresh at a market. This is because most fast-food restaurants fry the helpful nutrients out of foods that are typically nutrient-rich. Not all players have access to unprocessed food, so a vitamin and mineral supplement could be integrated into a healthy diet.

There are specific pills for a single vitamin or mineral that a diet is lacking. Multi-vitamins are supplements that contain a mixture of vitamins and nutrients.

A mineral or vitamin can be helpful in small amounts but become dangerous in large proportions. You can overdose on vitamins, which can result in a multitude of side effects that can be strange (your hands turning yellowish orange due to carrot juice) or downright terrifying (loss of vision, numbness, liver damage). Remember, you can have too much of a good thing! Talk to your doctor before taking any supplement.

Avoid Scams

Make sure when you buy a dietary supplement that it comes from a reputable source. Ask your physician, or pharmacist if a certain product can be trusted. In a study in 2004, scientists found that many products that claim to have creatine actually contain none. Even more alarming was that in a separate study in 2001, analysts found out that many chemicals were in muscle-gain products besides the ones that were advertised. Some even included steroids that are harmful to the body and banned from competitive sports.

CREATINE

Creatine is a protein that's found naturally in the body's muscle cells. When taken in larger doses than usual, creatine increases protein **synthesis** in body cells. Athletes who take creatine have more energy to exercise and can improve strength and speed during an exercise routine. Football players are often eager to get an extra energy boost from creatine, but this dietary supplement can have negative side effects, such as nausea and vomiting. Some specialists doubt the supplement's usefulness for long-term usage. Always talk to a doctor before taking creatine. Also, creatine is only suitable for adults; if you're under seventeen, you should not take it.

PROTEIN SUPPLEMENTS

As we said before, food is the best source of nutrients, and that includes protein (the nutrient found in meat and dairy products). Protein helps your muscles repair themselves—but immediately after a workout, you probably won't feel like eating a large, nutritious meal, and you may not have time immediately after winning a big game. Protein shakes can offer a quick fix in these situations. These products usually contain proteins, carbohydrates, and fats; some include vitamins as well. Drinking protein shakes after your workouts and games can help keep your muscles healthy.

   A **nutritionist** can help you fit protein shakes into your diet in the most effective way possible. Remember that protein shakes, if needed, can supplement a lack of protein intake. However, any shake cannot replace a balanced diet, no matter how many nutrients are in it.

AMERICAN

FOOTBALL

6
The Dangers of Performance-Enhancing Drugs

Understanding the Words

Hormones *are chemicals your body releases that give special instructions to your body. One thing that hormones do is tell your body how to develop sexually when you hit adolescence.*

Paranoia *is a mental disorder that causes a person to believe that others want to hurt him.*

Delusions *are a mental disorder where a person believes things that are not actually true.*

Lyle Alzado first began using steroids in college. As a small player in high school, he never achieved the scholarship of his dreams. Steroid use was an easy fix, a shortcut to success in football. Once he got to the NFL, the steroid abuse did not stop. At first there was no problem; he enjoyed a lucrative career in football and was very successful. As a player for the Broncos, Alzado played very well. His statistics were impressive, and he led his team to its first winning record in its history.

On the field, Lyle was on the top of his game, but off the field, life was getting out of hand because of his steroid use. He experienced spurts of violent rage at times and had to deal with the pains of mental addiction. Later, he

Using a performance-enhancing drug may seem like an easy way to get ahead of your competition. The truth is, though, that these drugs are illegal and carry a lot of side effects that are not worth the risk.

said, "I just didn't feel strong unless I was taking something." His personal life was in shambles and it never recovered. In March of 1991, he couldn't walk a straight line at his fourth wedding. He was diagnosed with brain cancer one month later. After a career of denials, Lyle went clean about his steroid use in an article with *Sports Illustrated*. While there is no medical link between steroid use and brain cancer, Alzado always believed that drug abuse was the cause. At 43, Lyl Alzado died of cancer.

Lyle Alzado's story shows both the perks and the ultimate downfalls of steroid use. It's all there: the initial success caused by taking performance-enhancing drugs, followed by the hard crash, first in a player's personal life, then on the field. The conclusion is obvious: performance-enhancing drugs just aren't worth it.

Supplement or Drug?

Specialists don't agree as to which "drugs" would belong in this chapter and which would belong in chapter 5, under nutritional supplements. For instance, if a player drinks a Red Bull before a game, is he abusing caffeine or is he taking a dietary supplement? While a medical specialist would agree that there is some grey area, they would all agree that the drugs listed in this chapter are much more of a danger to a player than dietary supplement abuse. Another large difference is that dietary supplements can either be used responsibly or abused, while any use of the drugs described in this chapter is abuse.

Types of Performance-Enhancing Drugs

Different types of performance-enhancing drugs dramatically vary in severity and in usage. They can be as simple as taking a caffeine pill before a game, or as complicated as an NFL player infusing himself with his own blood before a big game.

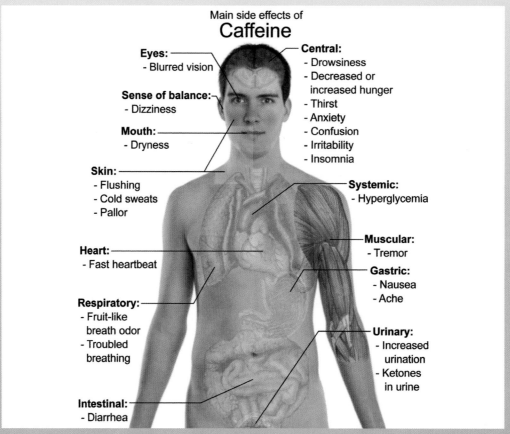

Main side effects of
Caffeine

Eyes:
- Blurred vision

Sense of balance:
- Dizziness

Mouth:
- Dryness

Skin:
- Flushing
- Cold sweats
- Pallor

Heart:
- Fast heartbeat

Respiratory:
- Fruit-like
  breath odor
- Troubled
  breathing

Intestinal:
- Diarrhea

Central:
- Drowsiness
- Decreased or
  increased hunger
- Thirst
- Anxiety
- Confusion
- Irritability
- Insomnia

Systemic:
- Hyperglycemia

Muscular:
- Tremor

Gastric:
- Nausea
- Ache

Urinary:
- Increased
  urination
- Ketones
  in urine

So many people (including athletes) drink caffeinated coffee or soda that it is easy to think of caffeine as no big deal. However, caffeine is a stimulant and can have negative side effects that may decrease your game day performance.

Difference Between Legal and Nonlegal Steroid Use

Steroids have legal and legitimate uses. After surgeries in which muscle tissue is lost, doctors may prescribe steroids to encourage muscle regrowth. After surgery for testicular cancer, men may be prescribed steroids to make up for lost testosterone. Steroids also help decrease inflammation.

Legal steroid use differs from illegal abuse in amount as well as purpose. Doctors prescribe much smaller doses of steroids than the athletes that abuse them. The typical steroid abuser takes eight to ten times the maximum recommended dose of steroids.

STIMULANTS

Before a game, football players sometimes use stimulants such as caffeine, as well as "uppers" known as amphetamines, to speed up brain activity. Stimulants increase alertness and aggressiveness.

Adderall is a stimulant widely abused among students to study, but athletes have also been known to abuse it. The Nevada State Athletic Commission banned athletes in the state from using Adderall, and the use of stimulants without a prescription is illegal in the United States. In 2009, the Saints kicker Garrett Hartley was banned from playing four games, not because he had taken Adderall for the actual football game, but because he took it to stay

awake on a long car ride. Football officials take Adderall abuse very seri-
ously, both on and off the gridiron.

STEROIDS

Steroids are the most common drugs abused by football players on any level
of play, including high school, college, and professional football. Steroid use
among high school students is a major problem that has doubled between
1991 and 2003. More than 6 percent of 15,000 students surveyed stated they
had taken steroid pills or injections. This means that across America and
around the world, thousands of teenagers are abusing steroids.

Athletes use steroids for many reasons. We live in a culture of easy fixes,
and it's hard to resist the allure of being able to bench-press an additional

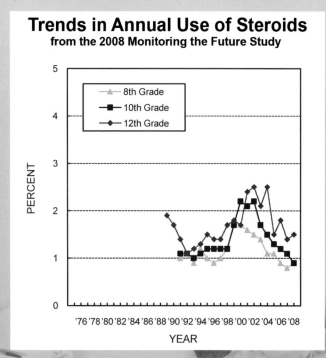

*The Monitoring the Future
Study is an annual survey of
adolescent drug abuse done by
the National Institute on Drug
Abuse.*

fifty pounds simply by taking a pill regularly. Another factor that contributes to steroid abuse is their availability. *Sports Weekly* held a discussion with high school athletes in the Washington area and found out that steroids were being openly used around the locker room and even cafeteria. Many coaches willingly turn a blind eye to steroid use, either because they approve of the effects the chemical gives to their teams or because they feel powerless to stop steroid abuse.

Negative Effects for Teens

While steroids take a terrible toll on the adult body, they cause even more damage to teenagers' bodies. The bones of a steroid abuser do not grow as much as they should, and the changes undergone through puberty can be accelerated. A teen who takes steroids before he is fully grown could risk being shorter than he would have been otherwise.

Severe acne, trembling, and high blood pressure are other side effects of steroid use in teens. Jaundice, which is a yellowish coloring of the skin caused by the liver not working correctly, is also a side effect, as is an increase in high blood pressure. In some cases, steroids can cause kidney and liver tumors in teens. Steroids affect **hormones** adversely as well; for males, steroids can shrink testicles and reduce sperm count, as well as cause baldness and breast development.

DID YOU KNOW?

Cigarette smoking is harmful for players on the field or off. Aside from the fact that an athlete dramatically decreases his agility and stamina by smoking (even during the off-season), cigarettes are extremely addicting. Cigarettes are the largest preventable cause of death in the United States. Statistically, smoking cigarettes is the most dangerous of all drug behaviors. Drugs as extreme as cocaine and as widespread as alcohol do not kill nearly as many people as tobacco products.

Potential Negative Side Effects of Steroids

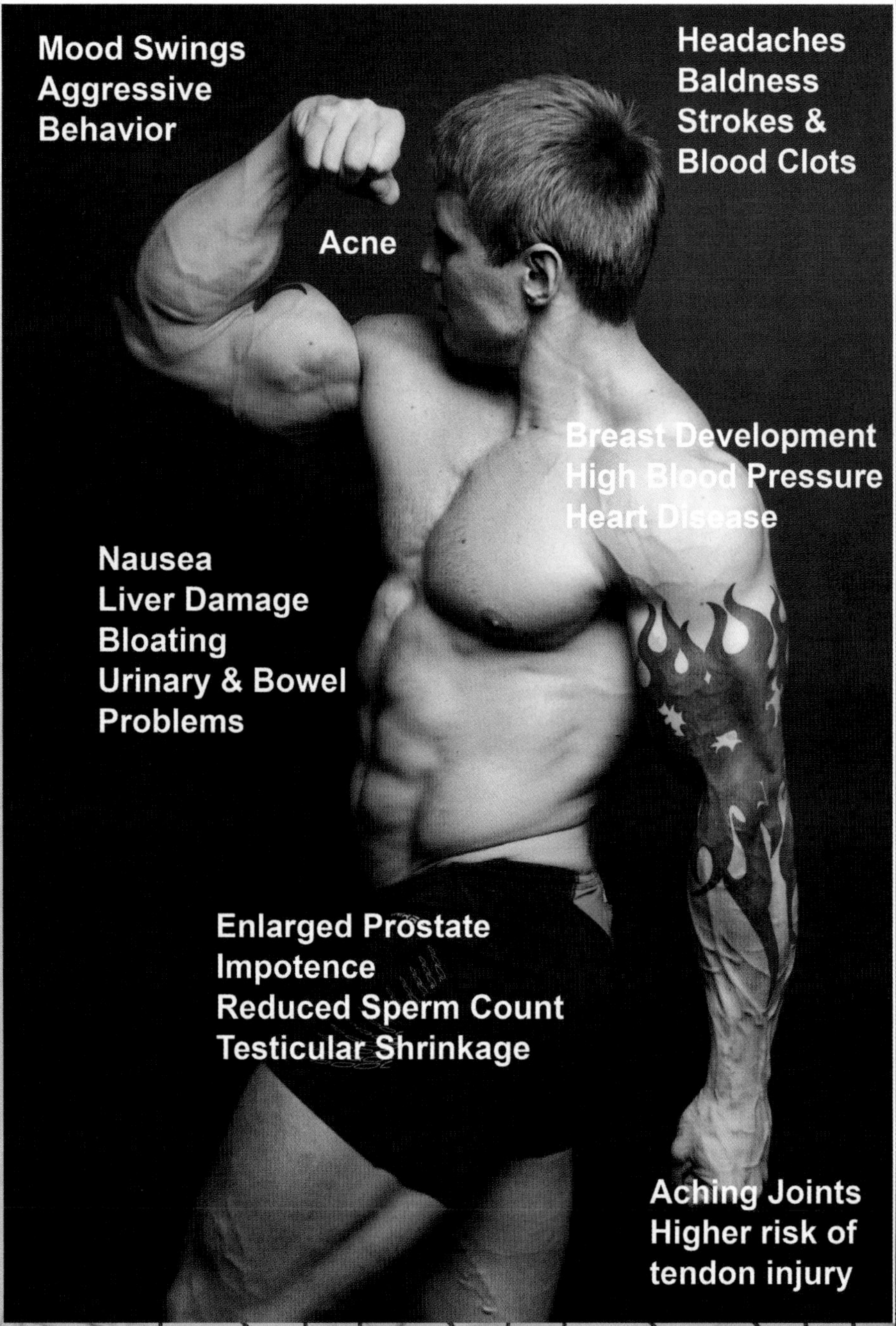

Mood Swings
Aggressive
Behavior

Headaches
Baldness
Strokes &
Blood Clots

Acne

Breast Development
High Blood Pressure
Heart Disease

Nausea
Liver Damage
Bloating
Urinary & Bowel
Problems

Enlarged Prostate
Impotence
Reduced Sperm Count
Testicular Shrinkage

Aching Joints
Higher risk of
tendon injury

A teenage athlete on steroids will also have a harder time coping with the emotional experience of growing up. While steroids make the athlete feel good about the size of his muscles, severe mood swings accompany this short-term confidence boost. Depression, sometimes even life-threatening depression, is often seen after steroids have been stopped. This makes steroids difficult to quit, like any other addictive drug. Other mental problems such as **paranoia**, **delusions**, and jealousy can accompany steroid use. Many guys taking steroids report a feeling of heightened energy and elevated mood, but this often creates what is commonly known as "'roid rage," where athletes who are dealing with a mix of increased testosterone and uncontrollable emotions go uncontrollably violent.

Alcohol and Substance Abuse

Many athletes feel pressured to party off the field. According to a study in 2009, 14 percent of athletes reported using alcohol in seventh grade, while by their senior year, 58 percent drank. Fewer athletes drink than non-athletes, but alcohol and street drug consumption is still a problem among student athletes, as well as professional players. Alcohol can impair reaction time on the field or in practice up to twelve hours after consumption. A player's potential to perform on the field is decreased by 11 percent if he abused alcohol recently.

Drinking off-season isn't the answer, either. Alcohol interferes with your muscles' performance. Hormones are also not able to kick in as well if a teen is drinking.

Steroids can cause many unwelcome side effects in young male athletes. Some side effects seen in women who take steroids include a deepened voice, increase in facial and body hair, reduced breast size and menstrual problems.

Life Lessons from Football

According to Coach Joe Maurelli, the most important lessons to be learned from football are:

- Learning to bond as a team: The sum of the parts is greater than the parts themselves.
- Understanding the definition of commitment.
- Understanding the concept of not giving up.

Quick Fix, Lasting Pain

Do you want to have catlike reflexes? Then do speed training and learn to prepare yourself mentally. Want to have huge muscles? Then choose your diet carefully and follow your coach's instructions. But taking performance-enhancing drugs just isn't worth it!

Sure, there are benefits for players who take steroids or stimulants in the short term. Otherwise, no one would take drugs. However, the risks involved with all performance-enhancing drugs are so extreme that taking drugs to perform on the field isn't just dangerous, it's ineffective. In the long run, these drugs do not help you play better. The fact is, performance-enhancing drugs destroy the body; they don't improve it.

Ultimately, life is more important than football. Drugs can damage your body, both on and off the football field. They can even take your life. They simply aren't worth it.

Drugs and Football

Colgate University's **Maroon-News** printed this story in September 2008, describing a disturbing connection between illegal drugs and professional football:

This summer, the most shocking, sensational and jaw-dropping story in sports went unnoticed. It had every aspect of a classic mafia movie: drugs, wired informants, even murder. **Sports Illustrated** writer Phil Taylor wrote that it was a story straight out of a "Martin Scorsese movie." Sounds like an intriguing lead, but no one seemed to care. But you should care, and so should the NFL.

Playing the role of the snitch in this saga is not Al Pacino, but New England Patriots' right tackle Nick Kaczur. An important starter in the Patriots 2006 AFC championship run, Kaczur was arrested in April for illegal possession of the prescription painkiller OxyContin. In June, the **Boston Globe** reported that Kaczur cooperated with federal authorities in an undercover sting operation. . . .

In another June incident, convicted steroids dealer David Jacobs and his girlfriend were found dead from bullet wounds in their Texas home. Just weeks before his death, Jacobs had supplied NFL investigators with a list of NFL players who had bought steroids from him, along with e-mails, checks, and other evidence that supported his claims. Jacobs explained his cooperation with investigators by saying he had made it his personal mission to "clean up the sport." Like in any good **Sopranos** episode, our first reaction is someone "took care of him." But police have yet to find any evidence of a hit and now believe it was a murder-suicide.

Both these horrifying and movie-like stories point to a disturbing drug culture in the NFL, yet the media and most Americans have somehow completely ignored these stories.

Final Note

Being a good football player requires much dedication and energy. Football players need to concentrate on being mentally and physically fit. They need to be mindful of eating habits and stay clear of needless supplements and dangerous drugs.

But there are other very important things you absolutely need to do if you're a football player: bond with your teammates, reach for your dreams, and enjoy yourself. In other words, have fun!

Further Reading

Dougherty, Jim and Brandon Castel. *Survival Guide for Coaching Youth Football (Survival Guide for Coaching Youth Sports Series)*. Champaign, Ill.: Human Kinetics Publishers, 2010.

Heisman, John. *Principles of Football.* Athens, Ga.: Hill Street Press, LLC, 2009.

Layden, Tim. *Sports Illustrated Blood, Sweat & Chalk: Inside Football's Playbook: How the Great Coaches Built Today's Game.* New York, NY: Sports Illustrated, 2010.

Stackmedia. *Football Training: For the Athlete, by the Athlete.* Chicago, Ill.: Triumph Books, 2009.

Find Out More on the Internet

"Are Steroids Worth the Risk" by TeensHealth from Nemours
http://kidshealth.org/teen/food_fitness/sports/steroids.html

National Collegiate Athletic Association (NCAA)
www.ncaa.org

National Football League
www.nfl.com

Sports Fitness Advisor
www.sport-fitness-advisor.com/football-training.html

Disclaimer

The websites listed on this page were active at the time of publication. The publisher is not responsible for websites that have changed their address or discontinued operation since the date of publication. The publisher will review and update the websites upon each reprint.

Bibliography

Answers.com, "The Crimson Tide," www.answers.com/topic/university-of-alabama-traditions?initiator=WANS#The_Crimson_Tide (26 January 2010).

AskMen.com, "Eating Well," www.askmen.com/sports/foodcourt_60/94_eating_well.html (26 January 2010).

Body Building, www.bodybuilding.com/fun/morgan5.htm (26 January 2010).

CNN, "Teen Drug Addicts," www.cnn.com/2009/HEALTH/08/26/teen.drug.addicts/index.html (26 January 2010).

Dial, Jenny, "No Sidelines for Him," Chron, www.chron.com/disp/story.mpl/sports/hso/6659439.html (21 February 2010).

Helium.com, "An Inside Look at Steroid Abuse," www.helium.com/items/396862-an-inside-look-at-steroid-abuse-in-college-and-high-school (26 January 2010).

History of Football, "First Super Bowl," www.historyoffootball.net/first_super_bowl.html (28 January 2010).

Maurelli, Joe, "The Power of Passion," www.askalana.com/stories/passion.html (21 February 2010).

Morrisville Chimes, "Super Bowl Fun Facts," media.www.morrisvillechimes.com/media/storage/paper1403/news/2010/02/05/Sports/Super.Bowl.Fun.Facts-3863758.shtml?refsource=collegeheadlines (26 January 2010).

Nutrition Data, "McDonalds Nutrition," www.nutritiondata.com/facts/foods-from-mcdonalds/6228/2 (26 January 2010).

PPOnline, "Stretching Factors," www.pponline.co.uk/encyc/0277.htm (25 January 2010).

Quote Garden, "Football," www.quotegarden.com/football.html (26 January 2010).

Raymond, Harry, "Drugs, Murder, and Football: The Problem the NFL Ignores," *The Colgate Maroon-News*, www.maroon-news.com/2.5268/drugs-murder-and-football-the-problem-the-nfl-ignores-1.802376 (21 February 2010).

San Francisco Chronicle, "Super Bowl Ads," articles.sfgate.com/2008-02-01/entertainment/17140446_1_super-bowl-bud-bowls-super-ads (26 January 2010).

Suellentrop, Chris, *Wired*, "Game Changers: How Videogames Trained a Generation of Athletes," www.wired.com/magazine/2010/01/ff_gamechanger/ (21 February 2010).

University of North Carolina, "Football Injuries," www.unc.edu/depts/nccsi/FootballInjuryData.htm (24 January 2010).

U.S.A. Today, "Steroids Report," www.usatoday.com/sports/preps/2005-06-08-sports-weekly-steroids-report_x.htm (26 January 2010).

U.S. Government, "Teen Drug Abuse Facts," teens.drugabuse.gov/facts/facts_ster1.php (26 January 2010).

Index

Picture Credits

About the Author and the Consultants

J. S. McIntosh is a writer living in upstate New York. He graduated from Binghamton University with a degree in English literature. He enjoys making music on his laptop, playing poker, and being a literacy volunteer. Currently, he writes on topics ranging from military history to health and fitness.

Susan Saliba, Ph.D., is a senior associate athletic trainer and a clinical instructor at the University of Virginia in Charlottesville, Virginia. A certified athletic trainer and licensed physical therapist, Dr. Saliba provides sports medicine care, including prevention, treatment, and rehabilitation for the varsity athletes at the university. Dr. Saliba is a member of the national Athletic Trainers' Association Educational Executive Committee and its Clinical Education Committee.

Eric Small, M.D., a Harvard-trained sports medicine physician, is a nationally recognized expert in the field of sports injuries, nutritional supplements, and weight management programs. He is author of *Kids & Sports* (2002) and is Assistant Clinical professor of pediatrics, Orthopedics, and Rehabilitation Medicine at Mount Sinai School of Medicine in New York. He is also Director of the Sports Medicine Center for Young Athletes at Blythedale Children's Hospital in Valhalla, New York. Dr. Small has served on the American Academy of Pediatrics Committee on Sports Medicine, where he develops national policy regarding children's medical issues and sports.